W9-BNJ-873

Dear Readers,

This is the story of a little girl who was taught to speak up for herself. She learned to be proud of who she was.

Because she respected herself, Rosa spoke out one day—and this changed many laws of our country.

Rosa sent a message to all—that all of the people in this world are equal and deserve to be treated with respect. We should all spread this message as we hold our heads high, just like Rosa Parks.

Your friend,

Garnet Jackson

Rosa Parks

Hero
of Our Time

Written by Garnet Nelson Jackson
Illustrated by Tony Wade

MODERN CURRICULUM PRESS

Program Reviewers

Maureen Besst, Teacher
  Orange County Public Schools
  Orlando, Florida

Carol Brown, Director of Reading
  Coordinator
  Freeport Schools
  Freeport, New York

Kanani Choy, Principal
  Clarendon Alternative School
  San Francisco, California

Barbara Jackson-Nash, Deputy Director
  Banneker-Douglass Museum
  Annapolis, Maryland

Minesa Taylor, Teacher
  Mayfair Elementary School
  East Cleveland, Ohio

Modern Curriculum Press
An imprint of Pearson Learning
299 Jefferson Road, P.O. Box 480
Parsippany, NJ 07054 - 0480

http://www.pearsonlearning.com

Library of Congress Catalog Card Number: 92-28583
ISBN 0-8136-5232-4 (Reinforced Binding)   ISBN 0-8136-5705-9 (Paperback)

17 18 19 20   12 11 10 09 08

When Rosa McCauley was a little
girl growing up in Pine Level,
Alabama, laws in this state
separated African Americans and
white Americans.

The adults could not work at the
same jobs. The children could not
go to school together.

·WHITE·

Many white people and black people were not friends. There were fewer blacks than whites. Often, blacks suffered greatly.

·COLORED·

This was the law.
This was the law
Of the land.
This was the law
That kept the South
Forever in shame.

3

Rosa was a tiny child, rather sickly and very frail. But she was always taught to stand up for her rights.

She lived with her mother, her younger brother, and her grandparents.

"Never let anyone push you around," her grandfather Sylvester always told her. And she never did.

Rosa's mother was a teacher. She taught Rosa how to read when she was only three years old. She also taught her how wonderful it was that she was a beautiful, smart, African American girl.

In school, as Rosa grew up, she was taught to hold her head high and to feel proud. And she did.

Rosa grew into a fine young lady. She met and married Raymond Parks.

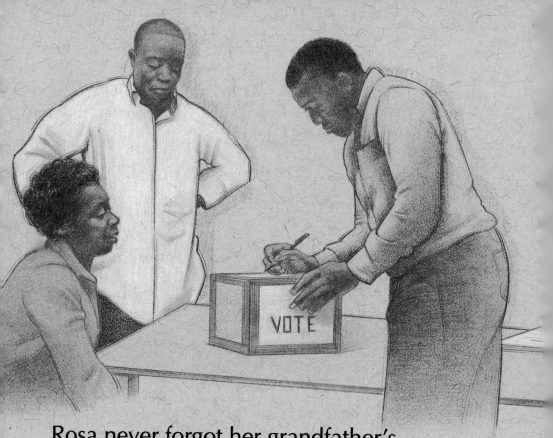

Rosa never forgot her grandfather's teaching to be brave. And she remembered the messages of pride and dignity of her mother and teachers. Together, Rosa and her husband worked to better the lives of her people. They helped many African American people who were treated unjustly.

She fought the law.
She fought the law
Of the land.
She fought the law
That kept the South
Forever in shame.

In 1955, Rosa and her husband were living in Montgomery, Alabama. She had a job sewing clothes.

One day after work she boarded a bus to go home. The bus became crowded.

THIS PART OF THE BUS
FOR THE COLORED RACE

12

When a white man got on the bus, there were no empty seats, so the bus driver told Rosa to give up her seat.

Rosa knew this was not fair. So with bravery and dignity, she said very softly, "No."

She fought the law.
She fought the law
Of the land.
She fought the law
That kept the South
Forever in shame.

The police were called. Rosa was arrested and taken to jail. This was December 1, 1955.

Rosa was released that night. But four days later, she had to stand trial.

Black people became very angry about this. Some white people were angry, too. They knew Rosa was right.

African Americans throughout Montgomery decided they would not ride the buses the day of the trial. Instead, they walked and they gave each other rides. They continued doing this for a whole year. This was called the Montgomery Bus Boycott.

18

Finally, the United States Supreme Court, the highest court in the nation, said that Rosa was right. African Americans could sit anywhere they wanted to on the buses. And they did not have to give their seats to white people. So, the boycott ended.

21

Rosa Parks's bravery helped make life better for all Americans. Laws throughout the South began to change. The way black people and white people felt about each other began to change, too.

They were more at peace with each other. They began to work at the same kinds of jobs and go to the same schools.

She changed the law.
She changed the law
Of the land.
She changed the law,
And no more
Was the South in shame.

She Changed The Law

One day in Alabama
Rosa boarded the bus,
A small quiet lady
Who wouldn't cause a fuss.

But she was told to move
And give up her seat,
So that a white man
Could get off his feet.

She was taken off to jail
Because she said,"No more."
And for Blacks in the South
She opened a door.

She started a movement
Throughout the land.
African Americans everywhere
Took a stand.

She changed the law.
She changed the law
Of the land.
She changed the law,
And no more
Was the South in shame.

Glossary

boycott (boi´ kät) The act of joining together in refusing to buy, sell, or use something

dignity (dig´ nə tē) The quality of being worthy; proper pride and self-respect

frail (frāl) Easily hurt, weak

message (mes´ ij) 1. A piece of news sent from one person to another. 2. An important idea that a person is trying to bring to others.

separate (sep´ ə rāt) To set apart from others

shame (shām) The feeling of losing the respect of others because of doing something wrong; loss of honor

suffer (suf´ ər) To feel pain; to put up with

unjust (un just´) Not just or right; unfair

26

About the Author

Garnet Jackson is an elementary teacher in Flint, Michigan, with a deep concern for developing a positive self-image in young African American students. After an unsuccessful search for materials about famous African Americans written on the level of early readers, Ms. Jackson filled the gap by producing a series of biographies herself. In addition to being a teacher, Ms. Jackson is a poet and a newspaper columnist. She has one son, Damon. She dedicates this book to the memory of her dear mother, Carrie Sherman.

About the Illustrator

Tony Wade is a graduate of the American Academy of Art and has worked as a commercial artist for over 10 years. He has illustrated many works, including *Cookies with Mrs. Flowers*, a children's book written by Maya Angelou. In *Rosa Parks*, Mr. Wade uses warm earth tones and strong lines to focus on a difficult moment in history.